What Would Jeff Do?

Inspirations from the World's Most Successful Ecommerce Company

By Greg Jameson

Published by WebStores Ltd.
www.WebStoresLtd.com
Franktown, CO USA

ISBN-13: 978-1511783842
ISBN-10: 1511783842

"If you like figuring things out, Greg Jameson gives you a lot to noodle on with this one. I'm on my second read already!"

"This Single Company Will Own the Future of Retail... the online giant is starting to stretch its entrepreneurial fingers into every retail segment, both online and off, making itself in effect a distribution company at heart. And why... because the founder, Jeff Bezos, is not only brilliant, and visionary, but most importantly he is willing to invest in the future 10-20 years out with no regard for Wall Street's happiness or unhappiness with the present. In my humble opinion they will make a last mile acquisition sometime soon... Lyft, USPS? Are you ready for an Amazon-centric world? As far as the bigger picture, my prediction is this: Amazon's global sales will surpass Walmart's within the next seven to 10 years."

Greg Jameson's book now answers the question-*How does Amazon do it?* In <u>*What would Jeff do?*</u> you'll jump into the brilliant mind of Jeff Bezos. By embracing and applying these principles anyone can succeed in business. This is a must read that unlocks the secrets of Amazon!

- Gary Barnes - Gary Barnes International
High-Performance Business Coach,
#1 International Author & Speaker

"Amazon is the most successful ecommerce website on the planet. Amazon has already spent millions of dollars determining what works and what doesn't. If you want to achieve success with your website, it only makes sense that you would emulate what Amazon does. Reading the quotes that Greg has compiled in this book provides motivation to follow Amazon's example for your business."

- Tamara Lowe, New York Times Best Selling
Author of "Get Motivated", Humble Servant &
Founder ChristianExperts.com

"Imagine, being able to pick the brain of the greatest marketing company on the planet, Amazon! Greg Jameson and his books will show you how you can effectively do just that!"

-   Brian G. Johnson
Serial entrepreneur, #1 best-selling author,
Founder MarketingEasyStreet.com

"OK. I must admit that I'm a quoteaholic. I've been collecting quotes for decades. Why? Because they are succinct nuggets of amazing wisdom from thought leaders much smarter than I. I'm simply smart enough to listen, learn and implement the ones that yell OMG-TIK (Oh My God-This Is Killer). Since Jeff Bezos is one of the brightest business leaders alive, I'm so excited that Greg Jameson has fed my quoteaholic habit with this delightful new book. Don't just read it. Study it. Find your own OMG-TIK nuggets and make yourself more money!"

Chasen Chess
Founder and CEO of Successful Lives Unlimited
Podcast host of Entrepreneur Marketing Mania

"This book went above and beyond my expectations. The short words of wisdom were easy and fun to read. It's one to treasure and keep. The words of wisdom from Amazon are vital for all current and future business owners. A must read."

Jessica Peterson
Founder, Customer WOW Project

"It's amazing how something the simplest easiest things to grow our business are right in front of our noses. In these days of launching, blogging, podcasts, SEO, and auto responders we think we have to be in the midst of technology to be successful - but Greg reminds us exactly what to put first, and some unique ideas that Jeff Bezos, founder of Amazon uses to keep the customer first and foremost front and center. Technology is great - but use it as a tool - not as the end game. You'll love the quotes to help keep you focus and also for quick inspiration."

Michelle Vandepas
Bestselling author and TEDx speaker
MichelleVandepas.com

"Have you ever wanted to sit down with someone as successful as Amazon's founder and CEO, Jeff Bezos, and listen to his advice on how to run a business? In, 'What Would Jeff Do?', Greg Jameson, the leading expert on marketing like Amazon, allows you to do the next best thing. This book is jammed packed with tidbits of information on what it takes to succeed online."

Steve Olsher
NY Times Best-Selling Author
Creator of several multi-million dollar companies
including Liquor.com

"Greg's short book on quotes from Jeff Bezos will save you a ton of money on an MBA. Study this book and you'll have a real world MBA in uncommon sense. Long-term success is always built on principles. And Greg's book clearly shows how no matter how much technology changes, delivering massive value is the key to greatness. Don't just read this book, study it. Great job, Greg!"

Kevin Knebl, CMEC
The Most Recommended Business Speaker in the World
Int'l Speaker/Author/Trainer and Executive Coach

"In Greg's new follow-up book to Amazon's Dirty Little Secrets, he nails the focus of Jeff Bezos and Amazon which is pleasing their customers so they will be more likely to market and promote Amazon's products and also shows how Bezos's intuition and long term thinking helps to reduce Amazon's risks to make it the powerhouse it is today. In "What Would Jeff Do" you'll learn what Jeff Bezos would do in short inspirational quotes. If you've ever wanted to get inspired from one of the world's top billionaires, read this book!"

Preston Rahn
Author, Coach and Sales Superstar
PrestonRahn.com

"We all know that "Success leaves clues", so I am sure that I am not alone in the intense desire to walk around the genius mind of Jeff Bezos, the creator of Amazon. "What would Jeff Do?" allows us to do this via a series of quotes, giving us the opportunity to read, ruminate, assimilate and integrate piece by piece the many golden nuggets that originate from Jeff himself. Many times when we read a book, we enjoy the contents but most of us rarely absorb them and consequently we infrequently apply them to our own business. Greg Jameson's book changes all this. So what would Andy do? He'd suggest you buy the book as he is certain you will thank him for doing so!"

Andy Shepherd
shepherdcoaching.com

Forward

When my book, "Amazon's Dirty Little Secrets" became a best-seller, I realized that lots of people wanted to know what makes Jeff Bezos tick. What are the secrets that has made Jeff so successful, and more importantly, how can you apply those to your business?

Lessons learned from Jeff Bezos – if you read "Amazon's Dirty Little Secrets" you may recognize the POWER+ acronym!

Plenty of Traffic. Amazon has an Alexa ranking of #4 in the United States and #7 globally. Interestingly, Amazon owns Alexa. But they certainly know how to drive traffic to their website. And the primary way they've done this is by getting others to talk about and promote their company. They accomplish this by having an unrelenting obsession with the customer. As a result, the customer sings its praises.

Amazon.com isn't just an internet success story. It's the standard by which all web businesses are now judged -- if not by their shareholders, then by their customers. Amazon set a high bar for reliability and customer service, and also introduced a wide range of online retail conventions -- from user reviews, affiliate marketing, and one-click shopping to the tab interface and shopping cart icon -- so commonplace we no longer think of them as once having been innovations. But these tools drive traffic while getting others to market on their behalf.

Offer Something of Value. In "Amazon's Dirty Little Secrets", this point is called "offer something for free", and while Amazon actually offers many things for free, the real way they get people talking about their company and spreading the word is because of the value they provide. So in this book, I've modified the point to discuss value.

One of the ways they do this is through innovation. Truly innovative products, services, and even delivery techniques attract the attention of the press and influential customers. Amazon is Amazon because they refused to use current paradigms as their starting point. Most of the time we use the well-worn phrase "Think outside the box." The problem with that type of thinking is that the box is still our point of reference. It is better for an organization to innovate, even if hurts your existing products or services.

Even when Amazon is not making dramatic changes or causing disruptive innovation, the company is constantly seeking to improve its existing systems. Continuous small improvements lead to major improvements, which increase the value to the customer.

Win Their Trust. When people can't see you or the product they are ordering, trust becomes one of the biggest factors with ecommerce. Amazon works hard to win your trust. I've never known a successful leader who did not expend years working hard. Sometimes we tend to think that there is a lot of luck in success. While there may be fortuitous circumstances, great leaders work hard to take advantage of them. Just eighteen years ago, Bezos was taking Amazon packages to the post office himself. "Complaining is not a strategy," says Bezos. A lot of energy has been expended complaining about Amazon. Many have said they have unfair competitive practices. Others object to the way they acquire companies. Great leaders don't waste time complaining about others. They use the precious resource of time to look to the future. As a result, customers trust them.

Engaging Experience. When it comes to customer experience, Amazon is a master. The biggest challenge for leaders is typically the balancing act between shareholder, employees, and customer. Jeff Bezos sees this differently; his sole focus is on customers. In fact, he's so emphatic about pleasing customers that he keeps an open chair in every conference room during meetings – that chair represents the customer. If the customer is happy, he believes that everything else will work-out in time.

If you are going to provide an engaging experience, you must stay focused on your areas of competence. It's difficult for a retailer to convince customers that they are also an IT company. Amazon started out as a retailer, but as they continued to grow, they quickly found new opportunities in other arenas. Inherently, the online business had many technical aspects, but as traffic to the site grew, so did their demand for processing and storage. In a short amount of time, Amazon found itself serving millions of visitors a day, and building a world-class computer processing and storage infrastructure. In an effort to maximize revenues, Amazon entered the commercial cloud computing market. This turned out to be an area of competence where they could provide a great customer experience.

Request an Action. The growth of Amazon is not a fluke. From the very early days, one of the mantras that Jeff Bezos continuously uttered was "Get Big Fast". They are a company that doesn't just sit around discussing possibilities – they take action on their ideas and they ask their customers to do the same.

Sometimes in business, the most important variable is beating your competition to the punch. This was something that Bezos understood and capitalized on. With the advent of the Internet, Bezos understood the potential of an online retail store that could sell anything, and the last thing he wanted was a missed opportunity. As a result, he instilled a culture within his company that speed was of the essence. Bezos's approach was more like, "let's own the market, and worry about the profits another day." The irony is Amazon now owns the online market, but the culture hasn't gone away.

✝ Additional Tips and Secrets. Because they do so many things well, Amazon has a large number of additional traits other companies can and should model. One of the traits Amazon is especially well known for its long-term thinking. Jeff Bezos like many other billionaires, are really long-term thinkers. Anytime he looks at a new business opportunity, he tries to see how that product/service might work in 10 years from now. From the very beginning, Bezos's plan was to have a store that could sell everything. Instead of trying to develop that grandiose model from the beginning, Bezos took the process in smaller steps. He reduced his risk for failure by just starting as a bookstore. He did this because there were only two major book distributes (Ingram and Baker & Taylor) in the US, and he found it easier to deal with just a few companies opposed to hundreds or thousands. In general, one of Bezos's greatest strengths was his ability to plan for the long-term future.

Another important trait that Bezos has is that he doesn't rely on intuition. Instead Amazon measures everything, and make their decision based on facts. By making decisions based on data, he minimizes the risks Amazon takes.

Take-aways on how to get others to market and sell for you:

- Stop worrying about the competition. Instead, put the customer first in everything you do. Build an awesome user experience and offer incredible value. When you do that, they will spread the word for you.
- Invent, experiment, and innovate with tools that make it easy for the customer to market on your behalf, such as affiliate programs and customer reviews. Continue to improve those tools until they are indispensable.

- Build trust by thinking long-term. Instead of worrying about how a customer return is going to impact your revenues, understand how that customer is going to influence others because you did right by him or her.

In the pages that follow, you will find quotes attributed to Jeff Bezos, the genius behind the "Everything Store", that reflect the principles described in the POWER+ acronym. I hope they inspire you to do what Jeff would do.

"I'm barely making ends meet. How can I start a business?"

*Our garage was basically
science fair central.*

I think I occasionally worried my parents that they were going to open the door one day and have 30 pounds of nails drop on their head or something.

I realized I'm never going to be a great physicist. That was where I was working when I came across the fact that the web was growing at 2,300 percent a year.

I'm going to do this crazy thing. I'm going to start this company selling books online.

It's highly unlikely and that started me thinking, 'What kind of business plan might make sense in that context of growth?

We've had three big ideas at Amazon that we've stuck with for 18 years, and they're the reason we're successful: Put the customer first. Invent. And be patient.

It's very important for entrepreneurs to be realistic. So if you believe on that first day while you're writing the business plan that there's a 70 percent chance that the whole thing will fail, then that kind of relieves the pressure of self-doubt.

That blank sheet of paper stage is one of the hardest stages, and one of the reasons it's hard is because at that stage there's nobody counting on you but yourself. Today it's easy because we've got millions of customers counting on us, and thousands of investors counting on us, and thousands of employees all counting on each other. In that beginning stage it's really just you, and you can quit any time. Nobody is going to care, so you set about doing the simple things first.

We are willing to go down a bunch of dark passageways, and occasionally we find something that really works.

For the first four years of the company, we worked in relative obscurity. We always had lots of supporters and we always had lots of skeptics, and that's still the same today. It's just that the level of visibility is so much higher. If you look at the six years that we've been doing business, in exactly one of those six years we were not the underdog.

When a company is very tiny it needs a tremendous amount of not only hard work but, as we talked about earlier, luck. As a company gets bigger it starts to become a little more stable. At a certain point in time the company has a much bigger influence over its future outcome and it needs a lot less luck and instead it needs the hard work. At that point there's a little bit more pressure, because if you fail you have nobody to blame but yourself.

*If you're not stubborn,
you'll give up on
experiments too soon. And
if you're not flexible, you'll
pound your head against
the wall and you won't see
a different solution to a
problem you're trying to
solve.*

*We're very comfortable
being misunderstood.
We've had lots of practice.*

"When we pioneered customer reviews, it was incredibly controversial. I got letters from publishers saying, 'You don't understand your business. You make money when you sell things. Take down those negative customer reviews.' We've never done anything of real value that wasn't at least a little bit controversial when we did it. But if you want to be a pioneer, you have to be comfortable being misunderstood."

"I very frequently get the question: 'What's going to change in the next 10 years?' And that is a very interesting question; it's a very common one. I almost never get the question: 'What's not going to change in the next 10 years?' And I submit to you that that second question is actually the more important of the two — because you can build a business strategy around the things that are stable in time."

"We know the energy we put into it today will still be paying off dividends for our customers 10 years from now. When you have something that you know is true, even over the long term, you can afford to put a lot of energy into it."

"The balance of power is shifting toward consumers and away from companies... The right way to respond to this if you are a company is to put the vast majority of your energy, attention and dollars into building a great product or service and put a smaller amount into shouting about it, marketing it."

The great thing about ideas is that every new idea leads to two more new ones. It's the opposite of a gold rush, where the more people who show up in 1849 to get that gold in California, the faster the gold runs out. Ideas are not like that; ideas breed.

A pioneering culture, one that actually enjoys and is excited by experimentation, a culture that rewards experimentation even as it embraces the fact that it is going to lead to failure — that is very important for larger companies in order to be entrepreneurial. And a long-term orientation is a key part of that. If everything has to work this quarter, then you're by definition not going to be doing very much experimentation.

You can't sit down to write a business plan and say you're going to build a multibillion-dollar corporation; that's unrealistic. A good entrepreneur has a business idea that they believe they can make work at a much more reasonable scale and then proceeds adaptively from there, depending on what happens.

*When the PR is good,
don't believe it; and when
it's the opposite way, don't
believe that either.*

"Be afraid of our customers, because those are the folks who have the money. Our competitors are never going to send us money."

"If you double the number of experiments you do per year you're going to double your inventiveness."

"We watch our competitors, learn from them, see the things they are doing for customers, and copy those things as much as we can."

"If you decide that you're going to do only the things you know are going to work, you're going to leave a lot of opportunity on the table."

"You have to be willing to be misunderstood if you're going to innovate."

"Frugality drives innovation, just like other constraints do. One of the only ways to get out of a tight box is to invent your way out."

Do I need to go down and get the certificate that says I'm CEO of the company to get you to stop challenging me on this?

"The great thing about fact-based decisions is that they overrule the hierarchy. The most junior person in the company can win an argument with the most senior person with a fact-based decision."

For every leader in the company, not just for me, there are decisions that can be made by analysis. These are the best kinds of decisions!

You can do the math 15 different ways, and every time the math tells you that you shouldn't lower prices because you're going to make less money. That's undoubtedly true in the current quarter, in the current year. But it's probably not true over a 10-year period, when the benefit is going to increase the frequency with which your customers shop with you, the fraction of their purchases they do with you as opposed to other places. Their overall satisfaction is going to go up.

One of my jobs is to encourage people to be bold. It's incredibly hard. Experiments are, by their very nature, prone to failure. A few big successes compensate for dozens and dozens of things that didn't work. Bold bets — Amazon Web Services, Kindle, Amazon Prime, our third-party seller business — all of those things are examples of bold bets that did work, and they pay for a lot of experiments.

Where you are going to spend your time and your energy is one of the most important decisions you get to make in life. We all have a limited amount of time, and where you spend it and how you spend it is just an incredibly levered way to think about the world. If you're going to spend time explaining the company, you should do it with people who are long-term investors, rather than traders. That's our point of view.

I work hard at helping to maintain the culture. A culture of high standards of operational excellence, of inventiveness, of willingness to fail, willingness to make bold experiments.

With annual planning processes, some companies literally start with, "Who are our three biggest enemies? Here's how we're going to hold them at bay or defeat them." We don't have such a list at Amazon. It's not how our annual planning process works.

I think we have been treated extraordinarily well by the press and the media — certainly by customers.

It's an essential job of any retailer to negotiate hard on behalf of customers. It's what we do.

It takes many hours to read a book. It's a big commitment. If you only think about books competing against books, you make really bad decisions. You're competing against Candy Crush and everything else. If we want a healthy culture of long-form reading, you have to make books more accessible. Thirty dollars for a book is too expensive.

In the internet era, almost all of the tools for reading have been reducing the friction of short-form reading. The internet is perfect for delivering three paragraphs to your smartphone. The Kindle is trying to reduce friction for reading a whole book.

At Amazon we like things to work in five to seven years. We're willing to plant seeds, let them grow — and we're very stubborn. We say we're stubborn on vision and flexible on details.

In some cases, things are inevitable. The hard part is that you don't know how long it might take, but you know it will happen if you're patient enough. Ebooks had to happen. Infrastructure web services had to happen. So you can do these things with conviction if you are long-term-oriented and patient.

We have a window of opportunity as larger players marshal the resources to pursue the online opportunity and as customers, new to purchasing online, are receptive to forming new relationships. The competitive landscape has continued to evolve at a fast pace. Many large players have moved online with credible offerings and have devoted substantial energy and resources to building awareness, traffic, and sales.

Our goal is to move quickly to solidify and extend our current position while we begin to pursue the online commerce opportunities in other areas. We see substantial opportunity in the large markets we are targeting. This strategy is not without risk: it requires serious investment and crisp execution against established franchise leaders.

We believe that a fundamental measure of our success will be the shareholder value we create over the long term. This value will be a direct result of our ability to extend and solidify our current market leadership position. The stronger our market leadership, the more powerful our economic model.

We first measure ourselves in terms of the metrics most indicative of our market leadership: customer and revenue growth, the degree to which our customers continue to purchase from us on a repeat basis, and the strength of our brand.

We will make bold rather than timid investment decisions where we see a sufficient probability of gaining market leadership advantages. Some of these investments will pay off, others will not, and we will have learned another valuable lesson in either case.

From the beginning, our focus has been on offering our customers compelling value. We realized that the Web was, and still is, the World Wide Wait. Therefore, we set out to offer customers something they simply could not get any other way.

Word of mouth remains the most powerful customer acquisition tool we have, and we are grateful for the trust our customers have placed in us. Repeat purchases and word of mouth have combined to make Amazon.com the market leader in online bookselling.

The right solution to sales tax in my view, and certainly this is Amazon's position and it's been consistent and we've had this position for 10 years, is that the right place to solve this is federal legislation.

If you're not stubborn, you'll give up on experiments too soon. And if you're not flexible, you'll pound your head against the wall and you won't see a different solution to a problem you're trying to solve."

"It's an all-you-can-eat buffet, $79, that gives you free two-day shipping on everything you buy for a year. When you do the math on that, it always tells you not to do it. While costs associated with Amazon Prime memberships and other shipping offers are not included in marketing expense, we view these offers as effective worldwide marketing tools, and intend to continue offering them indefinitely."

"Sometimes we measure things and see that in the short term they actually hurt sales, and we do it anyway."

"When you look at something like, go back in time when we started working on Kindle almost seven years ago…. There you just have to place a bet. If you place enough of those bets, and if you place them early enough, none of them are ever betting the company. By the time you are betting the company, it means you haven't invented for too long."

"If you decide that you're going to do only the things you know are going to work, you're going to leave a lot of opportunity on the table. Companies are rarely criticized for the things that they failed to try. But they are, many times, criticized for things they tried and failed at."

"If you're truly obsessed about your customers, it will cover a lot of your other mistakes."

One of the things we don't do very well at Amazon is a me-too product offering. So when I look at physical retail stores, it's very well served, the people who operate physical retail stores are very good at it…the question we would always have before we would embark on such a thing is: What's the idea? What would we do that would be different? How would it be better? We don't want to just do things because we can do them…we don't want to be redundant."

"If we think long term, we can accomplish things that we couldn't otherwise accomplish."

First of all, I think innovation is a point of view. You have to actually select people that are a part of the company who want to innovate and explore. Being a pioneering company and an explorer company isn't for everybody.

When you attract people who have the DNA of pioneers and the DNA of explorers, you build a company of like-minded people who want to invent. And that's what they think about when they get up in the morning: how are we going to work backwards from customers and build a great service or a great product? That's a key element to invention.

And that part is fun, by the way, so if you're the right kind of person and you like to invent, you like change, and everything you see as you move about the world you think how it could be improved, that's just fun and at Amazon over the last 18+ years has attracted a bunch of people like that and we have a ton of fun doing it.

Now there are area a couple of other things that are essential for innovation and invention that are not as fun. One of them is you have to have a willingness to fail. You have to have a willingness to be understood for long periods of time.

If you do something in a new way, and I don't care what it is, people are initially going to misunderstand it relative to the traditional way. And there will be well-meaning critics who generally want the best outcome but they're worried about this new way.

*And there will also of course be self-interested critics who have a vested interest in the traditional [way]. They have some profit stream tied to the traditional [way]. They have some profit stream tied to the traditional way... **If you never want to be criticized, for goodness sake don't do anything new**.*

When you have to write your ideas out in complete sentences and complete paragraphs, it forces a deeper clarity of thinking.

"We're not competitor obsessed, we're customer obsessed. We start with the customer and we work backwards."

We have so many customers who treat us so well, and we have the right kind of culture that obsesses over the customer.

Our point of view is we will sell more if we help people make purchasing decisions.

"If we can arrange things in such a way that our interests are aligned with our customers, then in the long term that will work out really well for customers and it will work out really well for Amazon."

You have to use your judgment. In cases like that, we say, 'let's be simple minded. We know this is a feature that's good for customers. Let's do it.

"All businesses need to be young forever. If your customer base ages with you, you're Woolworth's."

"In the old world, you devoted 30% of your time to building a great service and 70% of your time to shouting about it. In the new world, that inverts."

The balance of power is shifting toward consumers and away from companies...the individual is empowered... The right way to respond to this if you are a company is to put the vast majority of your energy, attention and dollars into building a great product or service and put a smaller amount into shouting about it, marketing it. If I build a great product or service, my customers will tell each other

Amazon.com strives to be the e-commerce destination where consumers can find and discover anything they want to buy online.

Because, you know, resilience - if you think of it in terms of the Gold Rush, then you'd be pretty depressed right now because the last nugget of gold would be gone. But the good thing is, with innovation, there isn't a last nugget. Every new thing creates two new questions and two new opportunities.

But there's so much kludge, so much terrible stuff, we are at the 1908 Hurley washing machine stage with the Internet. That's where we are. We don't get our hair caught in it, but that's the level of primitiveness of where we are. We're in 1908.

What we want to be is something completely new.

There is no physical analog for what Amazon.com is becoming.

It's our job every day to make every important aspect of the customer experience a little bit better.

We expect all our businesses to have a positive impact on our top and bottom lines.

Profitability is very important to us or we wouldn't be in this business.

The one thing that offends me the most is when I walk by a bank and see ads trying to convince people to take out second mortgages on their home so they can go on vacation. That's approaching evil.

You're not going to make Hemingway better by adding animations.

You know, we love stories and we love narrative; we love to get lost in an author's world.

The thing that motivates me is a very common form of motivation. And that is, with other folks counting on me, it's so easy to be motivated.

You want your customers to value your service.

What consumerism really is, at its worst is getting people to buy things that don't actually improve their lives.

The best customer service is if the customer doesn't need to call you, doesn't need to talk to you. It just works.

*On the Internet,
companies are scale
businesses, characterized
by high fixed costs and
relatively low variable
costs. You can be two
sizes: You can be big, or
you can be small. It's very
hard to be medium. A lot
of medium-sized
companies had the
financing rug pulled out
from under them before
they could get big.*

It is very difficult to get people to focus on the most important things when you're in boom times.

If you only do things
where you know the
answer in advance, your
company goes away.

The human brain is an incredible pattern-matching machine.

Percentage margins don't matter. What matters always is dollar margins: the actual dollar amount. Companies are valued not on their percentage margins, but on how many dollars they actually make, and a multiple of that.

Your margin is my opportunity.

Part of company culture is path-dependent - it's the lessons you learn along the way.

*My view is there's no bad
time to innovate.*

You don't want to negotiate the price of simple things you buy every day.

I went to Princeton specifically to study physics.

Email has some magical ability to turn off the politeness gene in a human being.

*You want your customers
to value your service.*

I wanted a woman who could get me out of a Third World prison. Life's too short to hang out with people who aren't resourceful.

There are two ways to extend a business. Take inventory of what you're good at and extend out from your skills. Or determine what your customers need and work backward, even if it requires learning new skills. Kindle is an example of working backward.

...one day you will understand that it is harder to be kind than clever.

If there's one reason we have done better than of our peers in the Internet space over the last six years, it is because we have focused like a laser on customer experience, and that really does matter, I think, in any business. It certainly matters online where word of mouth is so very, very powerful. If you do build a great experience, customers will tell each other about that.

You know if you make a customer unhappy, they won't tell five friends, they'll tell 5,000 friends. So we are at a point now where we have all of the things we need to build an important and lasting company, and if we don't, it will be shame on us.

Infrastructure web services had to happen.

We were hoping to build a small, profitable company. And of course, what we've done is build a large, unprofitable company.

We're taking no chances in marketing this holiday season.

A brand for a company is like a reputation for a person. You earn reputation by trying to do hard things well.

*If you don't understand
the details of your business
you are going to fail.*

The common question that gets asked in business is, 'why?' That's a good question, but an equally valid question is, 'why not?'

People forget already how much utility they get out of the Internet - how much utility they get out of e-mail, how much utility they get out of even simple things like brochureware online.

Market leadership can translate directly to higher revenue, higher profitability, greater capital velocity, and correspondingly stronger returns on invested capital.

It's not an experiment if you know it's going to work.

I've always been at the intersection of computers and whatever they can revolutionize.

The book is not really the container for the book. The book itself is the narrative. It's the thing that people create.

I strongly believe that missionaries make better products. They care more. For a missionary, it's not just about the business. There has to be a business, and the business has to make sense, but that's not why you do it. You do it because you have something meaningful that motivates you.

"If you're thinking about community-generated content, it's something we've always done. Listmania [customer lists of related products they like], customer reviews, wish lists. [We] may be inspired by these techniques, but maybe social networking is always a modest piece of what we do."

"We've never tested and we never will test prices based on customer demographics ... What we did was a random price test, and even that was a mistake because it created uncertainty for customers rather than simplifying their lives."

We were optimistic when we wrote our initial plan, but we've vastly exceeded those expectations. The key thing we have done and the reason we have been success if we've focused entirely on creating a value proposition for the customer.

"While free shipping is expensive for the company, it saves our customers tens of millions of dollars each quarter, and we plan to keep it in place indefinitely."

"Our vision first and foremost is to be the Earth's most customer-centric company and then, within that, to build a place where people can come to find and discover anything and everything that they might want to buy online."

"The earth's most customer-centric company is figuring out what the customer wants and how to give it to them ... By offering a universal selection of products, we can do something online that you could never do in the physical world."

"We invite authors to communicate with their readers in a way that hasn't before been possible. Amazon Connect brings the author's message to the reader instead of waiting for the reader to find the message."

"Thanks to free shipping and low prices, we expect more customers to turn to us for their holiday gifting needs this year -- producing our biggest holiday shopping season ever."

"This single individual completely changed something. That's the kind of thing people can do anywhere. They can do it in Seattle they can do it in North Dakota."

"This is an incredible and humbling honor. The Internet holds the promise to improve lives and empower people. I feel very lucky to be involved in this time of rapid and amazing change."

"A year from now Barnes Noble won't even consider us a direct competitor ... What we're trying to do is invent the future of e-commerce."

"We are very grateful to our customers for choosing Amazon.com as their online music store so quickly. We work hard to earn the confidence of our customers.

"In January, we shifted money from TV and print advertising to customers through lower prices and free shipping ... We're pleased with the results."

Everything you are comes from your choices.

Work hard.
Have fun.
Make history.

Strip malls are history.

I very much believe the Internet is indeed all it is cracked up to be.

Market leadership can translate directly to higher revenue, higher profitability, greater capital velocity, and correspondingly stronger returns on invested capital.

Invention is by its very nature disruptive. If you want to be understood at all times, then don't do anything new.

*Mediocre theoretical
physicists make no
progress. They spend all
their time understanding
other people's progress.*

For many people, extended reading sessions on an LCD display cause eyestrain.

*For people who are
readers, reading is
important to them.*

*People who are right most
of the time are people who
change their minds often.*

My own view is that every company requires a long-term view.

If you're very clear to the outside world that you're taking a long-term approach, then people can self-select in. As Warren Buffett says, you get the shareholders you deserve.

We want to make money when people <u>use</u> our devices, not when they <u>buy</u> our devices.

*I knew that if I failed I
wouldn't regret that, but I
knew the one thing I might
regret is not trying.*

The framework I found which made the decision incredibly easy was what I called – which only a nerd would call – a 'regret minimization framework'. So I wanted to project myself forward to age 80 and say, 'Okay, now I'm looking back on my life. I want to have minimized the number of regrets I have.

If you think about the long term then you can really make good life decisions that you won't regret later.

If you're competitor focused, you have to wait until there is a competitor doing something. Being customer-focused allows you to be more pioneering.

There are multiple ways to be externally focused that are very successful. You can be customer-focused or competitor-focused. Some people are internally focused, and if they reach critical mass, they can tip the whole company.

Failure comes part and parcel with invention. It's not optional. We understand that and believe in failing early and iterating until we get it right. When this process works, it means our failures are relatively small in size (most experiments can start small)., and when we hit on something that is really working for customers, we double-down on it with hopes to turn it into an even bigger success.

One of the huge mistakes people make is that they try to force an interest on themselves. You don't choose your passions. Your passions choose you.

Real estate is the key cost of physical retailers. That's why there's the old saw, location, location, location.

Your brand is formed primarily, not by what your company says about itself, but by what the company does.

*Cement. That's the perfect
product to sell at Amazon.*

We were profitable in December of 1995, but that is the worst mistake any company could have made.

This is a multi-decade process.

*We are talking about
getting 15% of the 5
trillion retail business.*

We're not going to raise prices. Don't hold your breath. We're going to lower prices.

You should listen to the customer, but you also have to invent for the customer. Like it was our job to invent One Click.

*It's hard to find things
that won't sell online.*

If you can't feed a team with two pizzas, it's too large.

Millions of people were inspired by the Apollo Program. I was five years old when I watched Apollo 11 unfold on television, and without a doubt it was a big contributor to my passions for science, engineering, and exploration.

What's dangerous is not to evolve.

If we can keep our competitors focused on us while we stay focused on the customer, ultimately we'll turn out alight.

*A company shouldn't get
addicted to being shiny,
because shiny doesn't last.*

Your brand is what other people say about you when you're not in the room.

*I don't know about you,
but most of my exchanges
with cashiers are not that
meaningful.*

When the world changes around you and when it changes against you – what used to be a tail wind is now a head wind – you have to lean into that and figure out what to do because complaining is not a strategy.

If you want to be inventive you have to be willing to fail.

In Seattle you haven't had enough coffee until you can thread a sewing machine while it's running.

I would define Amazon by our big ideas, which are customer centricity, putting the customer at the center of everything we do.

We see our customers as invited guests to a party and we are the hosts. It's our job every day to make every important aspect of the customer experience a little bit better.

I love slipping into a comfortable chair for a long read, as I relax into the chair, I also relax into the author's words, stories, and ideas. They physical book is so elegant that the artifact itself disappears into the background. The paper, glue, ink and stitching that make up the book vanish, and what remains is the author's world.

*I don't want to use my
creative energy on
somebody else's user
interface.*

It's so ambitious to take something as highly evolved as the book and improve on it.

There are two kinds of companies, those that work to try to charge more and those that work to charge less. We will be the second.

I'd rather interview 50 people and not hire anyone than hire the wrong person.

If you make customers unhappy in the physical world, they might each tell 6 friends.

If you make customers unhappy on the Internet, they can each tell 6000 friends.

This may look like science fiction. It's not...We can do half hour delivery for 86% of the items we carry...It will work, it will happen, and it's going to be lots of fun.

I want to see good financial returns, but also to me there's the extra psychic return of having my creativity and technological vision bear fruit and change the world in a positive way.

Things never go smoothly.

If I had a nickel for every time an investor told me this wouldn't work....

The Internet in general, and Amazon.com in particular, is still Chapter One. You're asking me about my story, and it's still the very beginning.

Make a
Statement!

Tell the world that you believe
in the wisdom of Amazon's business
model. Logowear is available at
http://www.cafepress.com/gregjameson

Special bonuses

Thank you for reading my book. In appreciation, I would like to offer you a physical copy of the companion book, my best-seller, "Amazon's Dirty Little Secrets" for free. All you do is pay a small shipping fee and I will send you an autographed copy when you visit:

http://webstoresltd.com/freebook

About the author

Greg Jameson has been involved in the computer industry since the mid 1970's when he was still in high school. He published his first commercial software program in 1985. After successfully taking his first company public, he has been developing internet applications since 1995 (essentially the beginning of the Internet). He has been creating ecommerce websites since 2002.

Greg has been named "International Developer of the Year", "Colorado Small Business of the Year", and listed on the Inc. 500 of America's Fastest Growing Small Companies. Today, Greg helps businesses through his company, WebStores Ltd where he provides Internet marketing services and builds customer-centric websites. Most recently, Greg's book, "Amazon's Dirty Little Secrets" has become a #1 Amazon Best-Seller.

Greg is available for keynote speeches, workshops, training, and seminars. Please visit GregJameson.com for details.